FEELINGS
Like Mine

Marie-Therese Miller

Special thanks to Stephanie Garrity, Executive Director of Rainbows for All Children

Lerner Publications ◆ Minneapolis

I feel thankful for John Edward, Michelle, Sean, Meghan, John Vincent, Erin, Elizabeth, and Greyson

Lerner Publications Company
An imprint of Lerner Publishing Group, Inc.
241 First Avenue North
Minneapolis, MN 55401 USA

For reading levels and more information, look up this title at www.lernerbooks.com.

Main body text set in Mikado a.
Typeface provided by HVD Fonts.

Editor: Allison Juda **Designer:** Emily Harris **Photo Editor:** Cynthia Zemlicka
Lerner team: Martha Kranes

OurFamilyWizard is proud to offer the Many Ways series. Since 2001, OurFamilyWizard has been dedicated to supporting communication between parents who are raising kids from separate homes. Over the years, the understanding of what a family looks like has changed. But no matter a family's shape or size, the meaning of family has always remained rooted in love and respect. We hope these books help children learn the many different ways to be.

Library of Congress Cataloging-in-Publication Data

Names: Miller, Marie-Therese, author.
Title: Feelings like mine / Marie-Therese Miller.
Description: Minneapolis : Lerner Publications, 2020. | Series: Many ways | Includes bibliographical references and index. | Audience: Ages 5–9 | Audience: Grades K–1 | Summary: "Feelings can be happy or sad, big or small, easy and hard, and everything in between. Explore a diverse mix of feelings and the many ways to tackle those feelings"– Provided by publisher.
Identifiers: LCCN 2019040525 (print) | LCCN 2019040526 (ebook) | ISBN 9781541598027 (library binding) | ISBN 9781728400143 (ebook)
Subjects: LCSH: Emotions—Juvenile literature.
Classification: LCC BF723.E6 M555 2020 (print) | LCC BF723.E6 (ebook) | DDC 152.4—dc23

LC record available at https://lccn.loc.gov/2019040525
LC ebook record available at https://lccn.loc.gov/2019040526

Manufactured in the United States of America
1-47993-48671-12/17/2019

Table of Contents

All Kinds of Feelings   4

Glossary   23

Further Reading   23

Index   24

All Kinds of Feelings

Everyone has feelings every day.
Some are **BIG**. Some are **SMALL**.

Feelings come and go. No feeling lasts forever.

You smile when you feel **HAPPY**.

You might feel **SAD** when your mom or dad goes away. It's okay to cry.

Grr! You feel **ANGRY** when your brother says mean things.

Take deep breaths, and count to ten. Soon you will feel **CALM**.

You might feel **SCARED**, such as on your first day of school.

Your friend is **NERVOUS** too. Talk about your feelings.

Sometimes you feel **DISAPPOINTED**.

Do something you love. Maybe try singing or dancing. You might feel **EXCITED** instead.

When you score, you feel **PROUD**. You run fast and stand tall.

When you feel **EMBARRASSED**, your cheeks burn. They turn red.

You feel **CURIOUS**. You have lots of questions.

You are ready to **LEARN.**

You lose the game. You feel **FRUSTRATED.**

Take a break. Then play again.

You feel **WIGGLY**. You want to move. Try a stretch.

You feel **TIRED**. Curl up and sleep.

You have **FEELINGS** every day.
FEELINGS are a part of being human.
They are all okay.

Glossary

angry: feeling upset or annoyed

calm: feeling peaceful and relaxed

curious: a desire to learn about something or someone

disappointed: feeling sad or unhappy because something was not as good as expected

embarrassed: feeling uncomfortable and ashamed

frustrated: feeling angry or upset because of not being able to do something

proud: feeling very happy or pleased because of something

scared: feeling afraid of something

Further Reading

Barnham, Kay. *Feeling Scared!* Minneapolis: Free Spirit, 2017.

Clark, Rosalyn. *Feeling Happy.* Minneapolis: Lerner Publications, 2018.

Feelings and Emotions
http://www.cyh.com/HealthTopics/HealthTopicDetailsKids.aspx?p=335&np=287&id=1530

Feelings Games
https://pbskids.org/games/feelings/

Jones, Grace. *My Feelings.* New York: Crabtrec, 2017.

Kreul, Holde. *My Feelings and Me.* New York: Skyhorse, 2018.

Index

angry, 8

curious, 16

excited, 13

frustrated, 18

happy, 6

sad, 7
scared, 10

wiggly, 20

Photo Acknowledgments

Image credits: Yuji Arikaway/Getty Images, p. 4; onkeybusinessimages/Getty Images, p. 5; MoMo Productions/Getty Images, p. 6; JGI/Jamie Grill/Getty Images, p. 7; Blend Images/JGI/Jamie Grill/Getty Images, p. 8; Inti St Clair/Getty Images, p. 9; fstop123/Getty Images, p. 10; kali9/Getty Images, p. 11; Jose Luis Pelaez Inc/Getty Images, p. 12; Peathegee Inc/Getty Images, p. 13; Pixel_Pig/Getty Images, p. 14; RichVintage/Getty Images, p. 15; Imgorthand/Getty Images, p. 16; Steven Puetzer/Getty Images, p. 17; JGI/Jamie Grill/Getty Images, p. 18; Hoxton/Paul Bradbury/Getty Images, p. 19; Wavebreakmedia/Getty Images, p. 20; Pollyana Ventura/Getty Images, p. 21; Ariel Skelley/Getty Images, p. 22.

Cover: digitalskillet/Getty Images (top left); monkeybusinessimages/Getty Images (top right); baona/Getty Images (lower left); DenKuvaiev/Getty Images (lower right).